Contents

Extreme changes	2
Recycling cans and plastics	4
The water cycle	8
Making crystals	11
Petrified lightning	14
Strands in action	16

Extreme changes

I think you have to control materials to an extent, but it's important to let the materials have a kind of power for themselves.

Keith Haring

Everything around you is made up of **matter**. Matter describes anything that takes up space. Matter can take different forms such as a solid (for example, a $1 coin), a liquid (a glass of milk) and a gas (the air that fills a balloon). The different forms that matter can take are called '**state**'.

When matter changes from one state to another, it goes through a **physical change**. This means that when you make water (liquid) into ice cubes (solid), you are creating a change.

There are two types of changes that can happen to matter:

Reversible changes: these changes can be undone so that the matter goes back to how it was before. For example, ice is water in a solid state. If you add heat to an ice cube, it will change back to liquid water again.

Irreversible changes: these changes cannot be undone to produce the same matter again. For example when you cook an egg, it cannot be changed back into its original form.

Did you know?
For a long time, people believed that all reactions were irreversible (that once something changed it couldn't be changed back again). It wasn't until 1803 that a French chemist called Claude Louis Berthollet discovered that some reactions were reversible.

LET'S FIND OUT

- What causes materials to change?
- What is a reversible change?
- What is an irreversible change?
- How do substances change state?
- How do materials change when they are recycled?

matter a physical thing that occupies space
state the way something is at a particular time (solid, liquid or gas)
physical change a change from one state (solid or liquid or gas) to another

This aircraft is travelling so fast it is causing a physical change in the air around it. The white cloud is formed by condensation; the exhaust and vapour from the jet hits the cold air and forms a cloud.

Recycling cans and plastics

Recycling involves collecting plastic, glass, paper and metal products. These products are then put through a number of changes to turn each type of material back into its original state.

Sorting

The rubbish in recycling bins is collected by garbage trucks and taken to recycling depots. Here, the rubbish is sorted and separated into different material groups, such as metals and plastics.

Recycling metal cans

Steel is a type of metal that is 100% recyclable. This means it can be used over and over again.

In Australia, 17.5 million steel cans are recycled each week.

Cans are made from different metals, such as steel and aluminium. Once the cans have been collected, they are sorted into their material type. Steel cans are removed from the huge piles of collected cans by using large magnets, which leave only the aluminium cans behind.

molten the liquid form of a material

The steel cans are put into a machine that squashes and flattens them. The flattened cans are packed into big cubes called bales. The bales are then taken to a metal recycling plant.

Cleaning

The bales of steel cans are shredded and washed in chemicals to remove any labels or dirt.

Heating

The clean steel is put into a hot furnace. **Molten** iron is added to the steel and hot air is blown into the furnace. Due to the very high temperatures (up to 1600 degrees Celsius) and the mix of oxygen, iron and steel, a physical change occurs. This change turns the hard steel into a runny liquid called molten steel.

Molten steel

Moulding

The molten steel is poured into moulds, which are then cooled with water. This cooling process turns the molten steel back into solid steel. The steel is then chopped into large blocks called slabs or ingots.

The steel blocks are heated to make them **pliable**. The softer steel can be made into sheets or coils.

This recycled steel is sent to factories where some of it is used to make new steel cans.

Making steel from recycled cans takes 75% less energy than making steel from scratch using **raw materials**.

Recycled steel can be used to make new things such as cans.

Recycling plastics

Plastics can be recycled and made into new plastic products. To do this, a recycling depot first squashes and packs their collected plastic into bales.

Bales (squashed cubes) of crushed plastic

Sorting and shredding

The bales of plastic are then taken to a plastic recycling plant, where the bales are broken up and sorted into different types of plastics.

The plastics are then shredded into tiny pieces called flakes. To separate the plastic from other bits of rubbish, such as glue and paper labels, the flakes are put into huge tanks of water called **flotation tanks**. The plastic flakes float on top of the water but the non-plastic rubbish is heavier and sinks to the bottom.

Washing and drying

The plastic flakes are washed to remove any leftover **residue**, such as dirt, labels or food that might still be mixed in with the flakes. The flakes are dried in a machine by spinning them at high speeds.

pliable easy to bend
raw materials materials in their natural form
flotation tanks large, enclosed tanks of water
residue small pieces that remain after the main part of something has gone

Heating

The clean plastic flakes are then heated, which turns them into soft and sticky molten plastic. It is pushed through a machine and comes out the other end of the machine in long, thin pieces.

Cooling

The long strands of plastic are cooled in water. Once they are cooled, the strands harden and are chopped into small pieces called pellets.

These plastic pellets will be used to make new plastic products.

The plastic pellets are sent along a **conveyor belt** and put into big storage drums. The drums of pellets are sent to factories where they are made into new plastic products.

Making new products

The pellets are heated, which causes them to join together into a runny, liquid plastic. The plastic is then used to make a range of different products. It can be poured into moulds to make cups and bowls, made into bottles by blowing air into it or pushed through special machines to make flat plastic sheets or pipes.

Conclusion

Heating and cooling are used to change materials from one state to another. Recycling uses a series of **reversible** changes so that a material can be reused to make new products, usually saving time, energy and the Earth's natural resources, and creating less landfill.

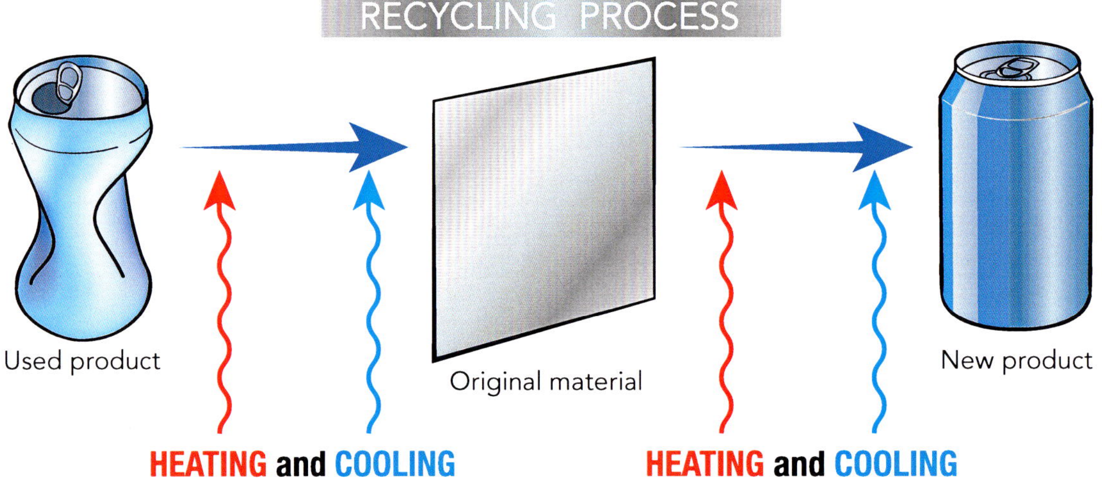

conveyor belt a continuously moving belt that carries objects along
reversible something that can be changed back to its original form

Breakaway tasks

Remembering

1 What happens when molten steel is cooled?

2 What happens when plastic flakes are heated?

3 On a T-chart, write three facts about recycling steel cans and three facts about recycling plastics.

Understanding

4 List the advantages of recycling materials such as steel cans or plastics.

5 Identify the reversible and irreversible changes that occur in the text. Write a definition for each of these words. Accompany each definition with an example from the text.

Applying

6 Using a flow chart, show the process of recycling either plastics or steel cans.

7 Research recycling practices. List five fascinating facts about ways to recycle a product that is not made of plastic or steel. Present your findings in a creative way.

Analysing

8 Compare the two ways in which steel cans and plastics are recycled. What things in each process are the same? What things are different? Present your findings on a Venn diagram.

Evaluating

9 Recommend changes that could improve the process of recycling cans or plastics. How can the process be made better, faster or more efficient?

Creating

10 You are Captain Recycle, a news reporter investigating the process and benefits of recycling. You are particularly interested in the changes that occur to materials during this process. Write a three-minute 'news flash' or write up an interview about your findings to present to your classmates.

The water cycle

Matter is found in three states: solid, liquid and gas. These forms are called the three states of matter.

Solids have a fixed shape, which is hard to change.

Liquids flow easily. They take on the shape of the container they are in.

A gas has no fixed shape or size. It spreads to fill the space it is in.

Water changes shape as it is poured from a bottle to fill a glass.

Some matter can change state depending on its environment. Water is a liquid at room temperature but it can also be changed into a solid (ice) or a gas (steam). These changes are reversible and can therefore happen more than once.

A clear example of these changes in state can be seen in the naturally occurring water cycle.

Water on Earth can be found as a liquid in oceans, lakes, rivers and creeks. It is found as a solid in ice glaciers. It is found as a gas in the form of water **vapour**. There are various conditions that cause water to change from one state to another.

vapour mist

Transpiration: when water is lost from plants through evaporation. In the water cycle, transpiration occurs when the heat of the Sun causes some water to evaporate from leaves, stems and flowers of plants.

Precipitation: when water falls to Earth from clouds. This happens when water droplets fall as rain (a liquid) or as snow (when the water freezes and becomes a solid).

Condensation: when a gas changes into a liquid. In the water cycle this happens when water vapour cools down, condenses and changes into tiny droplets of water. Millions of these tiny water droplets join together to form clouds.

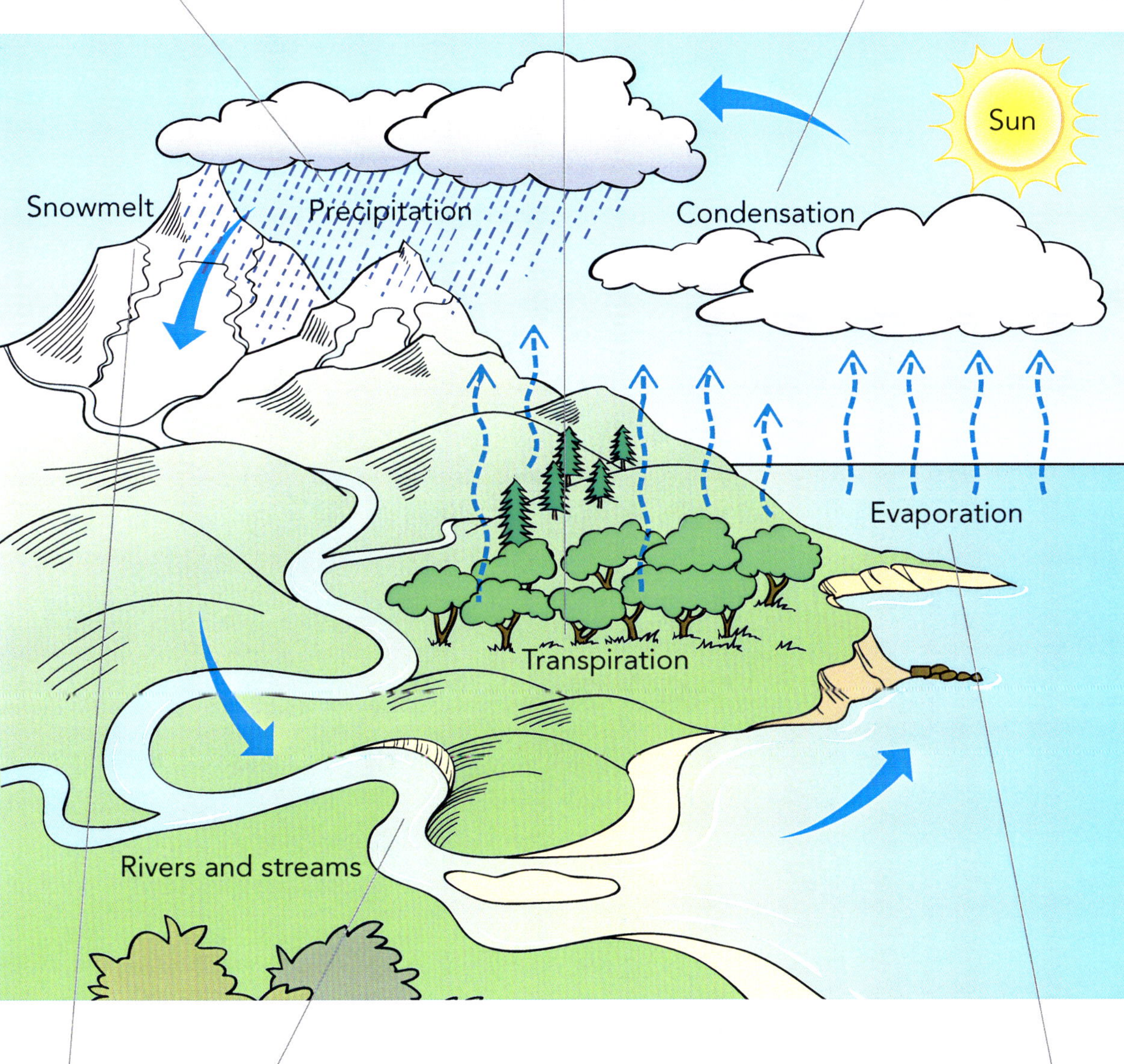

Snowmelt run-off: when ice on a mountain is heated by the Sun, it melts to become water and trickles down the mountain into small streams. The streams run together to form rivers, which run into lakes or flow out into the ocean.

Evaporation: when a liquid changes to a gas. In the water cycle, this happens when the heat from the Sun causes the water to evaporate into a gas called water vapour. The water vapour rises up into the air and forms clouds.

condenses when a gas cools and becomes a liquid

Breakaway tasks

Remembering

1 Identify the three states of matter. Draw and label an example of each.

2 Define 'evaporation'.

3 Draw and label two different types of precipitation that occur in the water cycle.

Understanding

4 Describe the changes that occur in the water cycle. Identify the conditions that are responsible for the change during each stage.

5 Complete a KWL chart about the water cycle. Investigate one question you have recorded.

Applying

6 Create and conduct an experiment to test whether evaporation or transpiration takes place in your schoolyard. Use the following headings to complete a report on your experiment:

- Aim
- Materials
- Method
- Observations
- Explanation.

Analysing

7 Look at the diagram that shows the water cycle on page 9. Why do you think this information has been presented in a circular diagram rather than in a linear (straight-line) flow chart?

Evaluating

8 Identify which parts of the water cycle affect our water supply. What weather patterns/conditions are ideal for good water levels?

9 What do you think would happen if one of the processes in the water cycle stopped working? List an example that shows your thinking.

Creating

10 Using a range of materials (leaves, grass, twigs, cotton wool, cellophane etc.), create a poster that explains the processes involved in the water cycle.

Experiment

Making crystals

Mixing, heating or cooling matter can sometimes cause it to change.

Some of these changes are reversible, while others are not. 'Irreversible change' means that once the material has changed state, it cannot be changed back again to its original form.

The experiment below explores one example of reversible change.

Aim

To observe a reversible change to a material

Materials

- ½ cup boiling water
- ¼ cup sugar or salt
- 1 pencil
- 1 polystyrene cup
- 1 spoon
- string (cotton or twine)
- 1 paperclip
- marker or paper tape
- heat-resistant gloves

Method

1. Carefully pour the boiling water into the cup. Ask an adult to help with this step, as it is always important to be careful when working with hot water.
2. Mark the water level on the cup using a marker or paper tape.
3. Add the sugar or salt and stir continuously with the spoon until the **crystals** dissolve.
4. Tie one end of the string around the pencil and tie the other end to the paperclip.
5. Sit the pencil on top of the cup so that the string and paperclip hang in the liquid.
6. Once the water has cooled, place the cup in a safe, warm spot such as a windowsill.
7. Each day for one week, observe the changes that occur.

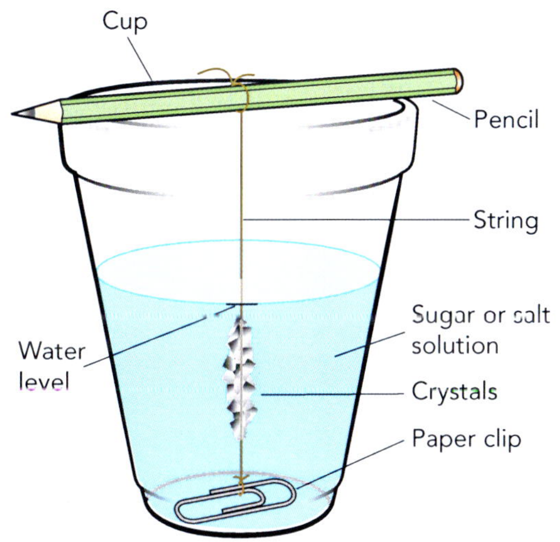

Experiment set-up

Safety tips

When dealing with hot water it is important to be careful. Always have adult supervision. Do not pick up the cup with your bare hands. Use heat-resistant gloves. Wait for the water to cool down before picking up or moving the cup.

crystals solids that have flat surfaces evenly arranged; usually transparent

Observations

During the week, the level of the **solution** will drop. Sugar or salt crystals will re-form and attach themselves to the string.

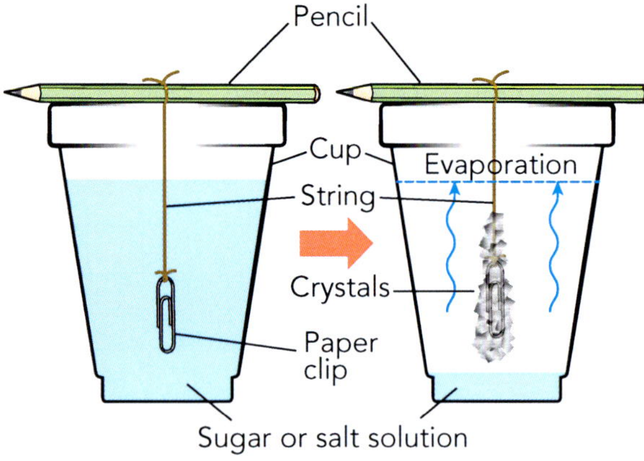

The experiment: before (left) and after (right)

Explanation

This experiment shows an example of a reversible change that involves two changes.

In this experiment, the first change occurs when the sugar or salt is dissolved in water. The second change happens when the sugar or salt re-forms back into crystals.

The material being dissolved is called the solute (in this case, the sugar or salt). The liquid used to dissolve a solute is called the solvent. In this experiment, the solvent is boiling water. When a solid is mixed with and dissolved into a liquid, a solution is formed.

Heat is better than cold for dissolving a solute. When sugar or salt is poured into hot water, the solution it makes can be described as **saturated**. This means that no more salt or sugar will dissolve in the water.

This experiment shows that the first change is reversible because the sugar or salt reforms into crystals.

This happens in two ways:

1. As the solution cools, it cannot hold as much sugar or salt as it did when the solution was hot. Some of the sugar or salt comes out of the mixture and reforms to make sugar or salt crystals.
2. Over time, the water in the solution evaporates (becomes a gas). As the amount of water decreases, the solution is less able to hold the remaining sugar or salt, so more sugar or salt crystals form on the string.

Sugar crystals

solution a liquid with a solid dissolved in it
saturated completely full of something; soaked

Breakaway tasks

Remembering

1 Name three materials used to set up the 'Making crystals' experiment.

2 How is a solution formed?

3 True or false? Sugar or salt crystals will form on the paperclip.

Understanding

4 Draw a set of labelled diagrams to explain each step in the method.

5 Explain why this experiment is a good example of reversible change.

Applying

6 With a partner and adult supervision, follow the method provided to conduct this experiment. Keep a diary of daily observations.

7 Create a flow chart showing the changes that occurred to the sugar/salt during this experiment.

Analysing

8 Investigate at least three other examples of reversible and irreversible changes to materials. Present your findings on a T-chart. Explain why each change fits in its chosen category.

Evaluating

9 Consider the following possible student observations:

a The sugar/salt didn't dissolve in the water.

b After one week, only a couple of small crystals had formed on the string.

Evaluate what you think went wrong in the experiment for these students. What advice would you give them?

Creating

10 Use the same method to investigate whether changes to a new set of materials can be reversible. Materials might include sand, flour, bicarbonate of soda, coffee and tea. First, note whether the materials are soluble in hot water. Next, photograph your results and record your observations on a data chart. Write a report about your findings.

Petrified lightning

Lightning has amazing powers. One bolt heats the air to 30 000 degrees Celsius. That's five times as hot as the surface of the Sun. Lightning can frighten pets, start fires, destroy trees and kill people. Lightning even has the power to make glass!

When a bolt of lightning strikes a sandy surface, the electricity can melt the sand. This melted substance combines with other materials. Then it hardens into lumps of glass called fulgurites. (*Fulgur* is the Latin word for 'lightning'.)

Now, scientists are studying fulgurites in Egypt to piece together a history of the region's climate.

Thunderstorms are rare in the desert of southwest Egypt. Between 1998 and 2005, **satellites** in space detected hardly any lightning in the area.

A fulgurite

Amid the region's sandy dunes, however, fulgurites are common. These lumps and tubes of glass suggest that lightning used to strike there more often in the past.

... The scientists, for the first time, also looked at the gases trapped inside bubbles in the glass. Their chemical **analyses** showed that the landscape could have supported shrubs and grasses 15 000 years ago. Now, there's only sand.

... Fulgurites and their gas bubbles are good windows into the past, scientists say, because such glasses remain stable over time.

... Even if you're afraid of thunderstorms, the amazing powers of lightning are bound to impress you! And lightning strikes can even tell a story of ancient times.

Source: Author Emily Sohn, *Science News for Kids*.

petrified when something has been changed into stone
satellites an object in the sky that orbits around a planet; satellites made by people are used to send and receive information
analyses investigations of things

Breakaway tasks

Science report

Remembering

1 How much heat can one bolt of lightning produce?

2 What does the electricity from the lightning do when it hits sand?

3 Where did scientists study the fulgurites?

Understanding

4 Write an explanation and/or draw a diagram to show how fulgurites are formed.

5 Identify the material that has been changed to create fulgurites. Is the change reversible or irreversible? Explain.

Applying

6 A reporter is interviewing a scientist. Write five possible interview questions that would help the reporter get the information they need to write the article on petrified lightning.

Analysing

7 What two main discoveries did the scientists make by finding the fulgurites? What evidence supported each discovery?

8 Research more about how fulgurites are formed. Record new facts on a concept map.

Evaluating

9 Evaluate the effectiveness of the article's headline and rate it out of ten. Give reasons to justify your rating. Create three alternative headlines.

Creating

10 Write a haiku or concrete poem about one of the natural elements mentioned in the article, such as lightning, sand, deserts or fulgurites. Present your poem in a creative way.

Strands in action

Core tasks

1 Choose a product, such as paper, glass, old cars or old computers that can be recycled. Research some facts about how this product is recycled. Create a poster showing the processes involved in the recycling of your product. Emphasise the changes that the materials go through. Give an oral presentation to the class based on the content of your poster.

2 Create a game to teach your classmates about reversible and irreversible changes that occur to different materials. Write out a set of clear instructions that explain how to play the game. Design a game board and create the required materials needed to play the game. Teach a friend how to play the game. Score the game out of ten for the following categories: fun, learning and creativity.

Extra tasks

1 Draw a labelled diagram showing something you have discovered about changes to materials. Write three questions that you would like to explore further about this topic.

2 Some words in this topic end in the suffix –tion, such as 'evaporation'. List these words and find out the origins of the suffix and its meaning. Add other 'tion' words to your list.

3 Write an article for the school newsletter that summarises what you know about changes to materials.

4 Investigate a change to materials that has not been discussed in the magazine. Write a radio interview between a journalist and an expert on this reaction.

When researching a topic, it is important that you understand what you read and 'paraphrase' or write your newly learnt ideas, using your own words. To check your understanding, use key words from the text to write a summary of what you have just read. Re-read your writing and add extra details to clarify your thoughts.